The Money Library Volume I

Living Great on What You Make

HEATHER D SCHOOLER

Published by: Servants Heart Publishing 2017

DISCLAIMER

The information provided in this material is for education and informational
purposes only, without any express or implied warranty of any kind, including
warranties of accuracy, completeness, or fitness for any particular purpose. The
Information contained in or provided from or through this material is not
intended to be and does not constitute financial advice, investment advice,
trading advice or any other advice. The information provided from or through
this material is general in nature and is not specific to you the user or anyone
else. You understand that you are using any and all information available on or
through this material at your own risk.

DEDICATION

TO HIM THAT IS ABLE TO DO
EXCEEDINGLY ABUNDANTLY ABOVE
ALL WE CAN ASK OR THINK.
&
IN MEMORY OF MY FATHER
WILLIAM B. SCHOOLER

I DEDICATE THIS WORK

MAY IT BE OF HELP TO ALL WHO
READ ITS PAGES

CONTENTS

ACKNOWLEDGMENTS

To my family. Those who kept me going
when all was falling apart, stood beside me
when things were going as planned, and
celebrated with me when things were better
than I could ever imagine.

INTRODUCTION

Welcome to the first step in living a great life with the salary you make. I am excited for you to read this book because I have a passion for helping people in the area of improving their money, their finances, and their processes.

My intention when writing this book was to provide you with a set of keys to enable you start the path to setting strong money goals that will allow you to learn how to live a full life both now and in the future.

The Money Library's future volumes will go into more specific detail about saving, your money personality type, investing, insurance, and entrepreneurship in a way that is easy to understand and implement. Congratulations to you for taking these first steps to financial freedom. I wish you great success on your journey.

CHAPTER ONE

MY STORY

From about the age of 13, my mom would allow me to help her with writing checks and paying the bills. Because of this, I had a small taste as to what our family's household expenses were like. When I got a little older, my mom would give me a signed check that I would take to the grocery store to buy the family groceries for the week (unfortunately we could not do this now because of identity theft and fraud).

Mom gave me a spending budget, which I usually went a little over. My mom never complained that I spent too much, she was very wise and let me learn. This small act allowed me to start learning some things from the family utilizing the family's money.

Ever since those days with the checkbook, I have been fascinated by the world of finance. How unfortunate it was when I graduated from college after all those years of education and coursework in accounting and business that the only advice that I really got, in terms of money and finances, was "Save as much as you can for retirement." My whole financial tool kit, learning and advice was summed up in one sentence from my mother.

Because there was no real reason behind the advice I was given, at 20, I did not really understand, "Save as much money as you can for retirement." In my mind I thought, "Why do I need to save now? I have plenty of time to save for retirement." Because I did not understand the reason why, I did the opposite and spent. Due to my lack of knowledge I put very little away during my first two years of work.

I was about 25 or 26 was when I started studying about money and finances. I had recently graduated from The Wharton School of Business with an MBA and approximately fifty five thousand dollars' ($55,000) worth of student loan debt. I was fortunate that right out of school I had a job and I was making a decent amount of money. Due to an increase in salary, I decided that it was the appropriate time to start investing for my retirement. At that time, I started to put a significant amount of money away in my 401k.

Though I was saving now, the next problem arose. I blindly invested, and did not understand what I was investing in. I was listening to the advice of others with no financial experience. All they could tell me was things like, "If you want to be aggressive, pick these. If you want to be conservative, pick these."

Here I am, this supposedly smart young lady with an ivy league MBA just randomly picking some mutual funds and hoping they did well. In reality, I had no idea what I was doing. Sometimes the funds performed well, and sometimes they did not.

I worked for a company at one point in my career that allowed me to buy stock at a discount. I purchased the stock, and later sold it, but I never understood what the benefit I would have later in life, if any. I was getting good at trying things at random with no rhyme or reason.

To learn more about investing and overall general financial health, I started reading books and taking classes, studying about money and finances. I wanted to learn more about the things that I was never taught because the school system and my parents did not know what to teach me.

I began to study more and I took a few of the classes that certified financial planners took. I got a few of my friends involved in an investment club. I continued reading and studying and finding out more about money.

My learning increased to the point that I began to realize that the reason people do not know anything about money is because parents and school systems do not teach anything about money. I also realized that, in general, people just did not want to talk about money, people did not want to learn about money, and it was causing many people I knew to be behind the curve in terms of their retirement and investing.

About five years, and I got the opportunity to volunteer to teach a class at my church on money and finances. When I found out the class was going to be offered, I immediately volunteered and was selected to be an instructor. When the time came, I was asked to attend training for another financial program, but after attending that training, I went back to the leaders who had sent me and said, "I am not going to teach this." I did not like the presentation of the material. The training was very basic material about savings and your credit, and it did not really encompass everything that I thought people should know. Things like how to fix problems and break failure cycles.

However when you come with a problem, you need to bring a solution. My solution was to create my own curriculum and I did that back in 2006. I have been teaching this curriculum and keeping it updated with things as they change, for example, the benefits of online banking, person to person electronic payments, and other new things that have taken place over the last decade.

Now that I have students that are like I was when I first started out on my journey, I have become fully invested in helping people improve their finances. Especially teaching individuals my financial curriculum. The more I taught, the more people began coming and asking me to help them with their finances, to one on one, to look at their situations, and to make recommendations.

I started to work with more people and I found myself in the financial coaching business. Since then, I have been coaching individuals and entrepreneurs, people who are looking to own their own businesses or quit their jobs so that they can get financially prepared. I want to spend my life doing this and be able to reach anyone who wants to improve their money and finances.

That is why I have written this book, and plan to write more. It is the reason why I have a curriculum, and why I am offering seminars across the United States and eventually across the globe. I want to reach as many people as possible and to get the word out that if you want to have good finances, if you want to be able to retire before age 70 or age 80, it is really possible.

I will show you some lessons in this book that will help make that dream a reality. All you need to do is make some changes to your lifestyle and some changes to the way you think. If you can do this you will have the ability to potentially enjoy life, not have to live in scarcity, and still be able to take your family on vacations and retire at a decent age, while having enough money to live on when you retire.

CHAPTER TWO

EXPENSE TRACKING

The first thing I recommend all people interested in creating good financial management habits do is to track your expenses. I have a two-tiered approach to this method which is different than what some other books may teach you.

Step 1: Spend only cash for the first 30 days. It has been proven that when people spend cash they tend to spend less money than if they use a credit or a debit card.

It has been proven that people actually spend less when they are handing out cash to a cashier or an individual versus when they are using a debit card or credit card. Which is one of the reasons it is easy to overspend with a credit or debit card. I want you to experience this by doing it yourself by spending only cash.

When spending, collect the receipts everywhere you go. You can collect the paper receipts and keep them in an envelope, you can take pictures of them, you can use an app or you can record anything that you purchase immediately onto your cellphone or tablet.

There are some good apps out there. Check the Apple or Google Play stores for the latest. Some that are popular include Level, Mvelopes, and Mint, but there are many apps that, at the time of writing this, have proven effective in helping people track expenditures.

If you do not want to go the electronic route, you can use pen and paper, an Excel spreadsheet, or anything that allows you to track all of your expenses. You will then add the receipts up at the end of the month and place them into spending categories.

I recommend you start at the very beginning of the month as that is usually the easiest. Start on the first of the month, and go to the last day of the month. If there are 31 days, go ahead and go 31 days instead of 30.

MONTH ONE CASH ONLY TRACKING

You will need cash since this is your cash spending month. Get about a weeks' worth of cash out of the bank to cover what you would normally spend on things that you would buy with your debit or credit card. Lunch, gas, coffee, every time you need more cash go to the ATM. Be sure to pay only cash for those types of things. I recommend having a minimum of one weeks' worth of spending money at a time to avoid having to run to the bank or ATM or paying fees from not going to your bank's ATM.

You can still pay your bills with online bill pay, but be sure to record this information on your choice of recording mechanism, paper, your computer, or the app. Get the rest of the money out in cash as you need it and use your cash to pay for your expenses.

Below is an example of what your tracking may look like. No matter what tracking mechanism you are using, be sure to categorize things. We will need to go back and sum things up by category at a later date.

Item	Amount	Category
Candy Bar	$ 1.50	Food
Bottled Water	$ 1.99	Food
Magazine	$ 5.97	Miscellaneous
Son's Lunch (Week)	$ 38.74	Food
My Lunch	$ 10.32	Food
Train Ticket	$ 5.95	Transportation
Gas	$ 20.00	Transportation

MONTH TWO DEBIT OR CREDIT CARD TRACKING

Step 2: For the second month or your next 30 days continue to track all expenses. However this time use no cash unless you absolutely have to. Spend only with a debit or credit card. When you are spending via debit card or credit card, you can tie the spending directly to the app and use it to create your receipts everywhere you go. Continue using whatever tracking mechanism you like. Record them with pencil and paper, Excel, or any other tools you desire to track your expenditures.

Oftentimes, if you are spending with a debit or credit card, your bank may even attempt to categorize the expenses for you or they will let you download the transactions in either a PDF an Excel format. This would allow you to easily track expenses as well.

It is very important for this to work the way it is designed, that you take the tracking very seriously. When I ask you to track everything, whether it is by cash for the first 30 days or by debit or credit card for the second 30 days, it is that you need to track everything. I mean **EVERYTHING**. If you buy a bottle of water out of the vending machine with a dollar bill, you need to track it. If you buy a hot dog at your son or daughter's hockey game, you need to track it.

Get a receipt for everything when you spend if it is not automatically electronically recorded so you will have the category to record later for the item. If they cannot give you a receipt, remember as soon as possible to write it down, put it in the app and record every single penny.

I can't emphasize enough that everything means every penny, dime, nickel, quarter, or dollar. If you give your kid two dollars and thirty five cents to buy a candy bar, you need to track the full $2.35 not just $2.00 or $2.50 but exactly $2.35. Every single penny you spend needs to be tracked, regardless as to whether it is a regular bill or it is just something that you bought on the spur of the moment. If you saw a young person with a lemonade stand and you bought a glass of lemonade or bought some Girl Scout cookies out front of the grocery store, you must still track it.

To get the best results, you must do this diligently. It is the little expenses that we tend not think about where we actually tend to accumulate a lot of money that we did not know we were spending. We can easily spend $2.27 here and $4.64 there and $0.75 here and a $1.50 on the bottle of water there. This detailed level of tracking is not overkill.

Step 3: Make sure that after you record all your expenditures that you log them by category. You will see a little more about the types of categories in the next section. For now, just make sure you group things together by like expense. Things like food, fuel, etc.

Step 4: After you have completed this tracking the next step is for you to compare your expenses for the cash spending days to your expenses for the credit spending days. We will look at them overall now, and talk about in the next section what you can do with all of that information that you have compiled, how you can analyze it and use it to improve your financial situation.

If you want to get results from this program, be sure for the next 60 days to make sure you collect every penny you spend. When you get the data, in the next chapter we will do a deeper dive and start looking at areas that we can improve.

Here is a miniature example of what a comparison chart might look like between cash and credit/debit month. Note that where there is an N/A there is no way that you can change the amount of the bill by paying cash versus credit. Paying cash will not affect the amount of the bill itself and can provide no savings. You could potentially turn your heat down in the winter to save money or car pool to work, but those types of savings we will discuss in the next section.

Item	Cash	Debit	Difference (negative is cash savings)	Category
Groceries	$ 276	$ 329	$ (53)	Food
Gas for Car	$ 297	$ 286	n/a	Gas
Coffee Out	$ 134	$ 192	$ (58)	Food
Electric Bill	$ 102	$ 89	n/a	Utilities
Totals	$ 809	$ 896	$ (111)	

To wrap up this section.   Here is a summary of your first exercise:

Step 1: Spend one month completely with cash, keep all receipts and track all expenses.

Step 2: Spend a second month doing the same thing with your debit card or credit card. Only spend cash when there is no other option. Track all your expenses.

Step 3: Group similar expenditures together like food, clothing, and utilities

Step 4: Compare your expenses for the cash spending days to your expenses for the credit spending days. See if you spend less when you were spending cash or credit

The best results come to those who are able to make tracking a habit. I have asked you to do this for 60 days, but long-term you will be ahead of the game if you make it a lifestyle.

CHAPTER THREE

CREATE YOUR UNIQUE PLAN

Congratulations. Now your expense tracking is completed, and everything is charted out. You have either put it in the app or you have put it in an Excel spreadsheet or you have written it down. Now it is time to create your budget.

I personally like the words "financial plan," but I also use the word budget because I know it is more commonly recognized. A budget to me means, "This is what I can and cannot spend." On the other hand, a financial plan means, "How I can make the money that

I have go as far as possible? What is my plan for my money?"

Living on a financial plan is probably one of the single most important things you can do to help get your financial house in order. Make this a habit and you will have a strong financial future.

Financial planning gives you control over your money instead of your money having control over you. Financial planning helps you make decisions with good information. A financial plan for your money is important so you are not just spending money haphazardly. Financial plans change with time and should be constantly evaluated.

You want to plan financial things in your life so that you have control over how they turn out. For example, if you plan a birthday party and you send out invitations several weeks prior to the party, the majority of the people you invited will be available to show up on that particular day and time. The party will be a success and everyone will enjoy themselves.

On the other hand, if you do not plan the birthday party, but instead call people up one hour before you want to get together, most of the people you invite will be unavailable or even if they are free, because of the short notice, they may choose not to come.

It is the same with your money; if you wait till the last minute or if you spend it haphazardly, you may not have the money available for the things that you really truly want to do. For this reason it is important to make sure that you have a solid financial plan put together. Preplanning allows you to have the party where all your friends show up.

Step 1: The first step in creating your financial plan is to document your income. Your income is any money that you receive from any source. The most common source is your income from employment, but you may also be getting an insurance payment, some type of payment for child support, maybe alimony, maybe some type of government assistance, unemployment, whatever the case may be. If it is money that you are receiving on a regular basis, this is considered income.

Step 2: Secondly, we are going to put down all of those expenses that you tracked for the 60 days. Expenses are everything you pay out. There are two key types of expenses. The first type is called *fixed expenses*. These are the ones that you do not directly control because the amount is set that you pay for these items. Examples of these include rent, fixed rate mortgage, and car/home/life insurance.

A fixed expense requires you to pay the same amount for a fixed period of time. Often times this fixed period will be a year or six months depending on the item. You may pay your car insurance every six months, you may pay homeowners insurance once a year, you may pay your life insurance policy once a year, garbage may be quarterly. In summary, fixed expenses are bills for things that have amount that doesn't change. They can be due monthly, quarterly, bi-annual, or annually.

Variable expenses are the second type. These are the ones that you have some control over and that can be adjusted without making a major change. Variable expenses are those that you are able to adjust. You could do this by moving to a less expensive place, getting a new car insurance company, or refinancing your car payment. Examples of variable expenses include things like food, entertainment, clothing, electricity, and other utilities.

Step 3: It is time to take all of our fixed and variable expenses and annualize them. What that means is to take them all and sum them up to a total amount you expect to pay approximately for the entire year. If it is a variable expense and you are unsure what the annualized amount would be, you have two options. The first is to take an average of the expenses. The second is to look at your records of what you paid last year and use that total number as an estimate for what you will pay this year. Select whichever you feel will be the best estimate of what you will pay for each bill over a twelve month period.

Since you have two months' worth of expenses already tracked, if you don't have your old records, you can multiply these expenses by six to turn that into an annualized number. To convert other items such as bi-annual expenses we would multiply them by two because they only happen twice a year, and so on.

Step 4: The next step is to label or categorize all the expenses. We label "cable," "cell phone bill," "internet," and if the categories change a little over time that is okay. I put gas and electric together and call them utilities. I put cable and internet together, but how you do this is whatever works best for you to remember. Group as many like items as you can together for comparison. Food I might divide between eating out and groceries because the costs are significantly different. These are my suggestions, do what works best for you.

Step 5: Finally we take all of the information we have compiled and annualized and take our income in step 3. To be clear, I am referring to our annual income that we calculated in step 1 minus our annual expenses. This gives us a number that tells us what money we have left at the end of each month if there is any money left. If it is negative, that means that we are spending more than we are receiving. If it is positive, that means we are going to have a little extra money left to do some investing or fun things, and if it is zero then that means that you are spending exactly how much you are receiving.

Below is an example of a sample budget.

Income After Tax (Items Rounded to Nearest Dollar)

	Jerry's check	$2,724.00
	Tina's check	$1,935.00
Total Income		$4,659.00

Expenses

Charitable Giving		$ 750.00
Food		$ 500.00
Mortgage		$ 855.00
Sewer, Water, Trash	Monthly Average	$ 30.00
Cell Phone		$ 150.00
Electric & Gas	Monthly Average	$ 200.00
Gas	Auto	$ 120.00
Credit Cards		$ 100.00
Cable, Internet		$ 150.00
Medical Expenses		$ 75.00
Toiletries		$ 125.00
Clothes	Monthly Average	$ 30.00
Miscellaneous		$ 20.00
Car Insurance		$ 50.00
Car Maintenance		$ 75.00
Presents - Birthday's		$ 50.00
Entertainment		$ 30.00
Retirement Savings		$ 750.00
Total Expenses		$4,060.00
Remaining Income	Income - Expenses	$ 599.00

Below is a sample. Give it a try for yourself.

	Dollar Amount
TOTAL INCOME	
Expenses	
Charitable Giving	
Food	
Mortgage	
Sewer, water, and trash	
Cell Phone	
Electric and gas	
Gas for cars (monthly average)	
Credit cards	
Cable, Internet	
Medical Expenses	
Toiletries	
Clothes	
Miscellaneous	
Car insurance	
Car maintenance	
Presents-birthdays, etc.	
Entertainment	
Retirement savings	
10% savings	
Total Expenses	

Congratulations. You have created your first financial plan, what I call the "as is," or what your financial situation looks like today. Since we have completed the "as is," we can now take a look and see where we want and need "to be" and make some adjustments.

I will challenge you to revise your financial plan in a way that will enable you to have a little bit more money left at the end of the month than you are actually spending. If at all possible, revise the plan so that your spending includes the 10% for savings and any money you are using for investing. Include these as expenditures in your plan.

While re-examining the plan, find out ways to tweak it to make sure that your number ends up positive or at a minimum, zero. There are a couple of strategies you can follow. One choice is to find way to cut expenses. For example, cut out that coffee from Starbucks and make coffee at home or lower your cell phone bill or cut off your cable and switch to Netflix, whatever you choose.

Your other choice/alternative to cutting back is the option of increasing your income. Depending on the size of your financial deficit a simple way to do this is to get a part-time job. I had a part time job for a while. When things were tight for me financially, I became a secret shopper to earn a little extra money on the side. The type of job is not important, you can get a part-time job at a department store, sell Mary Kay or some other home-based business while you continue to work full-time. Overtime, if available to you, can help you save massive amounts of money. I have a friend who worked for the State. He knew people at his job that doubled their income by working overtime every year.

I have a client who owns a fitness center, and we figured out for her, the best way to increase her income, to pay for all of her expenses, was to get more clients. So we set a goal for her to get a certain number of clients in a year, and then that would enable her to take care of the business in the way she felt comfortable, where she would not have to worry about paying any of the bills out of her own personal expenses.

Now it is time to determine which option you will choose. Will you increase your income or you can decrease your expenses? I prefer the increase your income option because to me, that seems to be a more flexible option in terms of being able to enjoy all of the things that you are currently enjoying in life and not changing your quality of life. However I understand this is not always and option because of life or family obligations. A the end of the day you want to make sure that there is cushion within the parameters of your budget so that you are able to live without stress and financial concerns.

To create a plan to pay off your debt, be sure to make it a goal. This is covered later in this book in chapter eight. One of the first things I would recommend as a long-term goal is paying off any consumer debt you may have.

I highly recommend against paying just the minimum to your credit card companies. If you look at your statements they will tell you how many years it will take you to pay off your card if you only pay the minimum and charge nothing else to the card. The numbers can be shocking. Depending on your debt and your interest rate, it could be ten years or more.

I recently saw a statement where it would take 18 years to pay it all back. On top of that the amount of interest paid was 200% of what was borrowed when all was said and done. As an example, this would mean that for every $500 you charged you would pay back $1500 in total. That's expensive money! The amount of interest you would pay during that time could easily fund your retirement.

Step 1: Take your highest interest rate bill or largest amount (you decide) that is not your mortgage and add to the minimum payment any extra money you have remaining from your financial plan after your 10% savings or the amount you earn from your part time job that you have created. This will now become the new payment until your debt for the first bill is completely paid off. For this to work you cannot accumulate any more debt.

I have put together an example of what someone's debt may look like – a few credit cards, a mortgage and a student loan. Round one shows you paying your extra cash that you have identified from your financial plan on one credit card.

Item	Amount Owed	Monthly Payment	Interest Rate	Extra cash	New Payment
Visa Card	$2,000	$25	17.90%		
Master Card	$5,000	$50	18%	$150	$200
Discover Card	$7,000	$100	9.90%		
Macy's Credit Card	$3,500	$25	22%		
Student Loan	$15,000	$300	6%		
Auto Loan	$20,000	$350	5%		
Mortgage	$150,000	$1,200	5.80%		

Step 2: Continue to pay the amount you have earned and put in your financial plan that is over and above the minimum payment until this bill is paid off. Below we show an example of where we apply the money to the card paid off to the next card you will be paying off.

Item	Amount Owed	Monthly Payment	Interest Rate	Extra cash	New Payment
Visa Card	$1,500	$25	17.90%		
Master Card	$0	$0	18%		
Discover Card	$6,000	$100	9.90%		
Macy's Credit Card	$1,750	$25	22%	$200	$225
Student Loan	$13,000	$300	6%		
Auto Loan	$18,000	$350	5%		
Mortgage	$148,000	$1,200	5.80%		

Step 3: Move to the next highest interest rate card. Now pay the same amount that you were using as a payment from the last card and apply that along with this minimum payment. This is called the snowball effect.

In round three we add to next card the cash you were paying on the prior two cards for an increased pay off for the current card.

Item	Amount Owed	Monthly Payment	Interest Rate	Extra cash	New Payment
Visa Card	$1,200	$25	17.90%	$225	$250
Master Card	$0	$0	18%		
Discover Card	$5,000	$100	9.90%		
Macy's Credit Card	$0	$0	22%		
Student Loan	$12,000	$300	6%		
Auto Loan	$17,000	$350	5%		
Mortgage	$146,000	$1,200	5.80%		

Step 4: Continue this process until all bills are paid. The last bill to be snowballed should be your mortgage as long as it does not have a prepayment penalty. If your mortgage has a prepayment penalty you may want to consider refinancing it so that you can increase your payments. Another option is refinancing from a 30 year to a 15 year mortgage. This will depend on a number of factors including how much you still owe. If your credit score is an issue, there are online resources at www.themoneylibrary.com to help you improve your credit.

It is important that you understand that debt payoff is a process and does not happen overnight. It may take a few years to pay down all your debt. To do this successfully, the key is to not accumulate new debt in the process of paying off the old. You do this by saving your 10% and paying yourself first while controlling your spending habits over time.

I would like to interject that for financial stability it is really critical that you pay yourself first. What I mean by that is, make sure that you have money set aside for yourself, to be able to eat, to be able to spend on things that you know you are going to need on a monthly basis or on an annual basis. I consider this extremely important because many people will feel harassed by someone they owe money to, or having to pay credit card bills and their student loans, and then not have any money for themselves to eat or pay rent.

I would never suggest to a person not pay a bill, but you are no good to the credit card company if you are unemployed because you could not get to work because you did not make your car payment. Call your creditors before this becomes an issue and talk to them. Most of them are willing to work out something to help you make it.

When you pay yourself first, I want you to understand that if you are in debt and your income is more than your expenses, this does not mean to buy yourself luxury items, only necessities. If you cannot afford the basic necessities, work on the debt reduction plan and work more to generate income to get yourself out of the vicious cycle called debt.

I know it may have an impact on your credit score if you do not pay your credit card bill, but it is going to directly impact your life if you do not take care of your basic needs: your food, your clothing, your shelter. Make this a time to communicate with your debtors and make a change that will allow you to make sure that the necessities are taken care of first.

In summary for this chapter, Step 1: Save an extra 10%; use this to invest. **Step 2:** Create your plan. Have your income listed and then all of your expenses. Make them annual. Once you have completed the annual plan, go ahead and divide that by 12 so that you can get a good idea of approximately what you are going to spend every month.

Step 3: Redo the plan. If you like where it is, that is great. If you have enough money coming in and a little bit left over at the end of the month, fantastic. I recommend a quarterly review, and a minimum annual review of your financial plan.

Step 4: If needed, prepare your debt reduction plan. Use chapter 8 to help you set a long-term goal to be debt free.

If you need help with any of these items please feel free to reach out to one of our coaches at The Money Library. We will work with you on your plan and answer any questions you may have about paying off debt.

CHAPTER FOUR

HIDE YOUR MONEY WISELY

Wherever you work, if you have availability, use direct deposit. Most of the time, employers will give you the option to direct deposit into more than one account. Direct deposit means that your check is automatically put in the bank and you do not get a hard copy paper check, which is the case for most places of employment now. If this is an avenue that is available to you, my recommendation is that you immediately start taking steps to save your money.

Except in cases of extreme debt, no matter your financial situation, you should start by saving (hiding) 10% of your income in a special account. Some might say, "10%? That is a lot!" However, if you think about it, it is only a dime for every dollar. You can afford to give yourself a dime for every dollar.

The purpose of this saving is to have money put away for something special you will need or want later, whether it be an emergency, or to buy your friends something great for Christmas. Whatever the case may be, we want to start this "hidden money" account so that you can take advantage of not seeing the money and learning that saving money is easy.

Step 1: Open up a second bank account. Note: If you do not have a first bank account – open one! This is critical to your ability to save and invest. For the most part, everyone in America can easily open a bank account.

Step 2: Complete any pertinent direct deposit information from your place of employment to have the money transferred when you get paid into the new account. To understand what paperwork is required, check with your Human Resources Department for the necessary instructions.

Step 3: Take 10% before taxes of your check and have that go into this extra account.

Special Tip 1: Do your research. Make sure this new bank account is one where you do not need to have a certain balance. Perhaps a credit union or a bank where just your direct deposit going in will allow you to not pay any monthly fees. This is critical. No fees.

Special Tip 2: If at all possible, do not have this account at the same bank that you currently have your savings or checking accounts. This is because when you log in on your phone to see how much money you have in the bank, you do not see this account. It is a "hidden money" account. This is very important because if you look at it, you are going to want to spend it. Also, you will start to see the balance get big, and think, "Oh, I can use that for something." We want to hide that money away so it is out of sight, out of mind.

Have you ever been surprised by finding lost money in your pocket? You had a coat, and you put your coat away for the winter, spring, and summer came, and fall came, and now it is winter and time to pull your coat out again. You put it on for the first time, and you stick your hand in the pocket, and you just find a $20 bill, and you are excited because you did not know that money was still sitting in your coat pocket.

If you learn to hide your money from yourself, the same thing is going to happen with your money when you do this direct deposit. It is like you got out those jeans that you had not worn in a long time, and you stuck your hand in your back pocket, and you found an extra $10. You will be able to experience that exciting feeling when you need to find this money, and then you remember you have it when you need it. Instead of that feeling in the pit of your stomach that asks, "How am I going to fix my car now?" you will get the exciting feeling that says, "Hey! I have that extra money to fix my car!"

In Summary:

Take 10% of your income and if possible use direct deposit to move it into an account at a bank that is not your primary bank. If you do not have direct deposit, set up a recurring payment from your first bank account to your hidden account electronically so it comes out on the day you get paid.

You will use this money for emergencies and to save for big ticket items. How much you should have saved depends on your financial plan, but I would recommend starting out with one month of your income and working your way up over time to one year of your net income. This becomes your safety net and no longer credit cards or other debt.

CHAPTER FIVE

DO NOT GO IT ALONE

It is critical for your success that you have someone who can hold you accountable. Find a reliable accountability partner. I have a couple suggestions of types of people that you can use to help hold you accountable. I would recommend when you are looking for someone to hold you accountable that you pick someone that is very disciplined in their own lives. This will give them a natural desire to hold you to the task.

Another option, if you have children, is to use your children. Children are great for this.

If you tell your children that you have a goal of tracking cash and receipts, you can make it a game, and say, "Hey, every time Mommy or every time Daddy goes somewhere, we have to get a receipt."

If you go somewhere and you do not get a receipt, your children will be in the backseat saying, "Hey, Mommy, you did not get your receipt" or "Daddy, you did not get your receipt!" The one downfall to this is they are typically not everywhere you are, and it typically doesn't work if your children are older (teenagers) or if they get bored with the game. You have to be creative with this strategy. It is a good way for them to learn good money habits by watching you learn yours.

Spouses, when you do the program together, are another great way to keep you accountable. This works best if both partners are committed to following the plan and succeeding. They both must commit to getting out of debt together.

If you are like me and do not have any children or a spouse to hold you accountable, it is okay. You still have other people to use for accountability. Be accountable to someone like your best friend or use a coach from The Money Library. When doing accountability with a friend or close family member like a spouse, it works best when the person holding you accountable is also doing the program with you.

If you are doing this with more than one person, the more the merrier. This is great to do with a group of friends. Especially when you are all doing the program at the same time.

If there is no one who you feel comfortable sharing this information with or going on this journey with, you can contact us at the Money Library and we will provide you accountability coaching to help you achieve your financial goals.

When you have someone who is expecting you to report to them that you did something toward your goals, you are a lot more likely to work on your objectives than if you are out doing it on your own. It is important that we can say to someone, "Hey, I would like for you to help me on this journey, and I am going to do 1 and 2 and 3 by this date. Will you hold me accountable?" Your accountability coach is going to ask you in a week or two, "How are you doing on Items 1, 2, and 3?"

If you are not having anyone hold you accountable, there is no one asking you how you are doing. And if there is no one asking you, then often times you do not get it done. You can go, "Oh, well, I will work on it next week" or "Oh, I did not get to it this week, so I will work on it next week." But, if you have someone who you know is going to ask questions, who you know is going to call you, who you know is going to send you a text or an email to check on you and see if you are going to accomplish these objectives, you are a lot more likely, even if it is just at the last minute, to make sure that you get this done.

You can use anyone you feel comfortable with, but we are here to help! The Money Library offers accountability coaching and video tutorials. If you are serious about taking your finances to the next level an accountability coaching package can help you speed up your journey. Just like a personal trainer helps someone move closer to their fitness goals, a financial coach will help you move closer toward your financial goals by having someone who is trained in their field help you achieve your dreams.

CHAPTER SIX

START RETIREMENT SAVINGS

Congratulations! You have done your tracking for 60 days, and you have all of that charted out. You know what you are spending your money on and this will help you to determine where you can cut back without significantly changing your lifestyle.

You have opened your new bank account and are now sending 10% of your income to this account as a savings vehicle. Finally, you have found an accountability partner or signed up for one through The Money Library and you use this person to help you keep on track with your tracking (pun intended). So, unless you are in the debt management phase that we discussed back in chapter three where your income is less than your expenses, then you are now ready for phase two of your master plan.

The next challenge is for you to save 10% more. Yes you read this correctly. This is not a typo. If your debt is under control then it is time to save another 10%. The reason for this is because the first 10% is for your emergency fund, for your fun money, for vacations, for your money that you may need to come up with to buy a new car or other expenditure, but this 10% we are going to use solely for investing in your future retirement.

I will give you a way to make this less shocking if you are not ready to jump in with both feet and do the whole 10% all at once. Start with 2.5%. No way you will miss 2.5% right? Next year go to 5%. The following year go to 7.5%, and then in year 4 move up to the entire 10%. This stair step approach still gets you to your goal. If you want to be an over achiever keep moving up your percentage by 2.5% each year until you are maxing out on the total amount you can invest per year. Which at the time of writing this book is $18,000 per year for anyone under 50 using a standard 401K program and $24,000 for anyone over 50.

Everyone who has paid off their debt, has a job or thriving business, should shoot for the goal to maximize their retirement because we want to work because we want to and not because we have to. This is achievable in America with hard work and dedication.

Why start early? Why not wait until you are older to start saving, and use this money for other things? The younger you start the less you have to save. It is something called the law of compound interest.

Let us look at some math. If you get approximately 6% interest on your retirement savings every year without withdrawing any money, just reinvesting it, how much do you need to save per month in order to reach $1 million by age 65?

Age you begin saving	Amount appoximately you must invest to reach 1MM by age 65
20	$ 350
30	$ 700
40	$ 1,500
50	$ 3,500
60	$ 15,000

Can you see the difference? If you start at age 20 your savings are almost half as much as if you start at age 30. But do not despair. If you are 40 and have not started, there is no time like the present. As you can see, based on the data, it is important that you begin to save for retirement as soon as possible to avoid having to work longer into your later years.

The goal for me is to enable all to work because we want to not because we have to. This gives us the ability to do other things like spend quality time with children, friends, and family, or travel the world. We will learn more about setting these types of goals in later chapters.

Most statistics show that unfortunately, most Americans have less than $1,000 in their savings account and in addition, most Americans under age 35 have less than $50,000 saved for retirement.

If we continue this way without pensions, people will have to continue to work because they will only be able to earn approximately $7,000 per year from the money they have saved for retirement. This trend has to stop, especially if you do not have a pension, and you have a company 401K program or even if you are an entrepreneur and have your own retirement plan.

The challenge is on for you to save for retirement. Out of every dollar you make, take out another dime, and invest this, either in your company's 401K program or a self-funded retirement program if your company does not offer a 401K. If you are self-employed you have the option to invest your paycheck in addition to some of the company's profits depending on the business type. I will get into more detail about the options available in the volume on investing.

There are a lot of great options you can choose from if you are self-employed or your employer doesn't offer a retirement plan. There are retirement plans called Individual Retirement Account or IRA. You can use an IRA to put your money into before tax if you have a business or corporation you own that can funnel money in, before tax.

Why do I care that the money is before tax? There are two arguments on whether you should invest before tax or after tax. I will let you decide for yourself which one you want to follow.

The before tax argument is based on the fact that you are able to defer your taxes for decades into the future where the total amount of income you will be earning is less than what you were making in your earning prime. The thought is that when you retire you will need less to live on because your major assets will be owned (house, etc.) and therefore you will need less money and if you earn less your taxes will be less.

The after tax argument is a simple one. We do not know what taxes will be like in 20 years. Therefore it is best to pay it now when we know, versus paying it later when taxes may be a flat 40% across the board. People who believe the government may raise taxes between now and when they pass on to the next world may want to pay taxes now while they are lower.

There are also after tax options based on your income level that you can invest in called a Roth IRA, which is an after-tax IRA, which means that when you retire, you only pay taxes on the gains from the account. One of the most fabulous ways to start off investing for your retirement is if the company that you work for has a 401K, 403B, or similar type of program where they do a company match, so check out your benefits, and if you do not know what they are, call your HR department and ask them.

If your company does a 401K match, what they are doing there is essentially giving you free money. Let me give you an example. Let us say your company matches dollar for dollar anything you put in your 401K up to $5,000/year. Because of this match, without even putting your money in a stock or a bond or a mutual fund, every time you put a dollar into this account, your company gives you a dollar.

Therefore, if you invest a dollar and your company gives you a dollar, you have doubled your investment. If you put in the full $5,000, you will get $5,000 from your company, which means that you have doubled your investment without having to do anything but put the money away. Who wants to turn down free money? I know I do not. So that is why I think companies with 401K programs, especially those that match, are the best places to start because a lot of times, they will give away free money or money for you taking the effort to put money in your retirement plan.

How do you find out if your company has a matching program or more information about your retirement options at your employer? Typically your human resources department will be able to tell you where to find this information and answer any questions that you may have. If your company does not have a retirement program, you can work with a bank or a company like Fidelity, TD Ameritrade, E*trade, Scottrade, and many others who will allow you to open your own personal IRA and invest your money.

CHAPTER SEVEN

LEAVING A LEGACY

Let us recap on all we have learned. Keeping in mind that you do not have to do all this overnight. It is a process. Take your time and do this properly.

Step 1: Track your expenses
Step 2: Create a financial plan
Step 3: Save 10% for family and emergency.
Step 4: Hide your 10%
Step 5: Save another 10% for retirement
Step 6: Do not go it alone

Once you have accomplished all the milestones in this book, I will make one final optional request for your consideration. Give another 10%.

Yes, I want you to save another 10% of your income, and this 10% I want you to give to charity or use it to leave something to your family. Some people may disagree with this, but I am firm believer that what you give comes back to you. So if you do not give of your money or yourself or your time or your energy to a worthy cause, then these types of things do not come back to you. I highly recommend this to everyone, once they become comfortable with their financial plan and they have a little money left over, take one dime out of every dollar and give it to a charitable organization of your choice.

It can be any organization that you deem is worthy or your money. It does not have to be a not-for-profit or a church or any type of specific organization. It just has to be someone or some company or some organization in need that you feel comfortable that if you were to give them money, that it would be put to use wisely. So I challenge you, as an accomplished saver and controlled spender, to put 10% away to give.

Become a game changer in the world, make a difference in the world, help those who are less fortunate, and really be appreciative of the things that you have been given in this life. Use what you have to help someone else have a better life.

Another way to give away this 10% (or more) is by leaving a legacy. This could be for your children, for your grandchildren, or for your nieces and nephews if you do not have any children. If there are no youths in your family that you would want to leave something, then you could leave money or your estate to a charitable organization.

There are lots of charitable organizations that have estate planning or estate giving programs, and individuals will work with you to set up bequeathing your estate or giving to their organization part of your estate when you pass on. Leave a legacy because we all know there are a couple of things that are guaranteed, death and taxes. When it is our time to go, no matter how soon or how far it is away, we want to make sure that we have made an impact on this world, not just by giving our 10% for charity, but also being able to leave a legacy or leave an inheritance to the next generation. We want to make people's lives better and to make the world a better place.

It is an honor and a privilege to be able to leave an inheritance to your children's children no matter how small. Far too often we know of churches or family members having to contribute to the burial of a loved one because they did not have the money left when they died for even their own burial. When most people die they do not want to be a burden on their family. It is also a great honor to be able to give to your family while you are alive.

Many people do not believe they will have an estate. But contrary to popular belief everyone has an estate. No matter how much or how little you have, everyone has something to leave and pass on to the next generation. An estate is any personal belongings that remain after you die, there are no size requirements.

Having understood that everyone leaves something behind, I will give you a few suggestions of how you may want to be remembered. However, as with anything personal, the choices are many and up to you.

First, I would mention leaving all or part of your estate to a charitable organization. Many charitable organizations will take their charitable donation when you pass away in the form of an insurance policy or another type of monetary donation that is payable upon your death. This is typically good for people who have extra to leave, beyond family, and who want to support an organization. This helps with reducing the estate costs for your family and allows you to be charitable at the same time.

If you are considering leaving something to your children, and you want to wait until you pass on, you may want to consider talking to a trust attorney about putting all of your items in a trust. That will allow you to more easily pass some of your wealth and real estate and things of that nature over to your family with the goal of "avoiding estate taxes." And what estate taxes are, are the money that needs to get paid to the IRS based on the value of what you have when you pass on.

If you are only going to leave very little, there will not be a lot in estate taxes or maybe none. If you are passing things onto your spouse, then you do not have to pay estate taxes as well. But there are many strategies that you can use to minimize the amount that you pay to the government legally and leave the most that you can to your children, your grandchildren, and your spouse.

There are insurance policies that you can get that will pass to your family members tax-free because insurance is not subject to estate taxes. And there are other things that you can do while you are still living, in terms of giving money to your children or grandchildren, so there is a gift amount, and at the time of writing, in 2017, it is $14,000 per individual. So you, as an individual, are allowed to give

If you are a married couple, then each parent can give to a child or to a grandchild for a total of $28,000 per year. So that doubles the amount that you are able to give tax-free. Now, the only caveat to this is the giving has to be while you are alive, but it is a great way to help children get through college or maybe get their first car, things of that nature. If you are giving them a gift for the year with the understanding that they do not have to pay income taxes; if it is both parents, $28,000, or if it is just one parent if you are a single mom or dad, it would be $14,000. But the key there is, this is while you are alive, but you are still leaving a legacy. You are still taking care of the next generation.

CHAPTER EIGHT

CREATING MONEY GOALS

When creating money goals the key is to **BE SMART ABOUT THINGS.** SMART is an acronym. All our goals should be SMART.

What is SMART?
- S = SPECIFIC
- M = MEASURABLE
- A = ACTIONABLE
- R = RELALISTIC
- T = TIME BOUTND

Smart goals are used to provide detail to what you want to have in your life. For example a SMART goal includes detailed things such as:

- New or used
- Pay cash or finance
- All the costs of a decision

Here are more examples of the SMART goals breakdown to help you to see how to set your own SMART goals.

S = Specific – Plenty of details about what you want
- For example:
    o Blue Kia Soul
    o Wi-Fi
    o Tinted windows
    o Black interior
    o Sound package
    o Extended warranty

M = Measurable – How will I know when it is completed?

- For Example:
  - I will own the home
  - I will have put away "X" dollars for my daughters college fund

A = Actionable - Something that I can directly control or take steps toward achieving.

- Save $50 per week – I have $50 to save

R = Realistic – Can I really do this task?

- Do I have the money?
- Do I have the time?
- Do I have the resources?

T = Time bound – How long do I have to get this task done?

- For Example:
  - Every year for the next 20 years
  - Within the next two years
  - In five years' time

Sample SMART goals can include things like:

- Buy a new Lincoln MKT costing $55,000 by paying $10,000 in cash down as initial expense within the next 2 years

- Research and open up a college fund to start saving for my child's college. Saving a minimum of $3000 per year for the next 10 years

STEP 1: Define Your Goal

Now it is time for you to determine what you want and write it down. Set your financial goals for the year and how you will achieve them. Do you want to be like the top 3% of the country? Then take the time and actually write out your goals and how you are going to achieve them.

Take some time to write out a few SMART goals for yourself using the notes pages.

Notes

Notes

STEP 2: Refine your goal

After you have written your SMART goals, continue to refine them by using the following criteria:

- What do you want to do specifically
- How much money do you need to accomplish this goal
- Before finalizing your goal – determine the hidden costs

Let us talk specifically about the hidden costs for major purchases. There are a few.
For example, let us say your objective is to buy a new car. What do you need to consider in terms of costs.

- Do you know how much new tires cost?
- Do you know how much an oil change is?
- Do you know how much your registration is annually?
- How much will your car insurance be?
- If you are getting a loan, how much in interest are you paying on that loan?

Example 2: Buying a house. Hidden costs could be things like the following:

- How much are the property taxes?
- How much is my private mortgage insurance?
- How much will it cost for maintenance on my home?
- How much will it cost to insure my home annually?
- How much will it cost for major repairs and do I have a fund set aside for that?
- How much will it cost me if I have a home owner's association fee?

If you have a fun long-term goal like a round the world vacation with your spouse:

- How much are passports?
- How much is airfare?
- How much is hotel?
- How much do we need to plan for spending money and including exchange rate conversions?
- Do we want to travel first class or go coach?
- How do we secure our home while we

are gone?

- Do we want to go with a group or travel on our own? What are the cost differences?
- How much is transportation while we are there?

Be sure to count all the costs. Not just the immediate purchase price, but the cost of maintenance and repair. Not just the cost of the airfare and hotel, but the cost of food daily and having to pay exchange fees at airports in each country you travel to. The risk of buying a home that you may not be able to sell for full value later. The price of buying a used car that has more problems than it was worth. There are risks to every purchase which people often fail to consider and these should be in the financial plan so that in case something does go wrong you are able to bounce back without issue.

Use the notes page to refine the goals you created before, or to make new and better ones.

Notes

STEP 3: Make it Bite Sized

Have you ever heard that old saying, "How do you eat an elephant? One bite at a time!" The same is true for your long-term goals. "How do you accomplish a goal? You must break down your major goal into short-terms goals or "chunks" or "pieces" you can manage and attain. This will help keep you encouraged and seeing progress as you move toward your goal.

Staying with our car example. If I want to buy that new car – a bite sized goal might be one or more of the following:

- Save $50 every paycheck for the next two months to put toward a down payment
- Keep all my spare change to apply toward my down payment
- Make coffee at home for the next 30 days and take the 3.50 per day and apply it toward my down payment
- Print out a picture of my car and put it on my vision board by next week

- Get online and model my car with all the features I want and save the photo on my desktop by the end of the month

Use the notes page to write down some of the short-term steps you will need to take to achieve your goal. I recommend writing down monthly and weekly objectives.

Notes

_____

_____

_____

_____

_____

_____

Notes

STEP 4: I AM

When you have refined your goal and have broken it down into actionable pieces and consider the goal is completed, take the final step and turn it into something that is in the NOW with an "I AM" statement. For example:

- I am the owner of a brand new Lincoln MKT
- I am the proud parent of a college graduate with no student loan debt
- I am enjoying Italy, France, and England with the love of my life

When you turn things into statements that start with I AM it helps you to visualize yourself in the place where you want to get. It allows you to imagine yourself already driving the car or sitting at your child's college graduation.

Write your "I AM" statements on the notes page.

I AM STATEMENTS

_____

_____

_____

_____

_____

_____

_____

_____

_____

_____

STEP 5: Write the Vision

It is time to take all your hard work and post it in your house or apartment. Post your I AM statements on mirrors and walls. Put your goals on colorful paper or use pictures to represent what you are going after.

Be creative in the way you display your goals. Attend a vision board or just create one yourself. Take photos and pictures from magazines or the internet to represent the dreams that you want to achieve.

There are vision board apps for your phones as well. You can set reminders to show you your I AM statements, or have your goals pop up on your tablet or phone.

Keep your dreams in the forefront of your mind. Think about them daily. Tell the people you trust that are positive and supportive of what you want to accomplish. Work on these with your accountability partner.

There is no dream to small or too big. Take advantage of this time to set the habit of creating goals for not just finances but for any dream you wish to have manifest itself in your future.

In summary, take these five steps to start on the path of creating your dreams.

Step 1:   Define your goal

Step 2:   Refine your goal

Step 3:   Make it bite sized

Step 4:   Create your I AM statements

Step 5:   Create your vision board

CHAPTER NINE

CELEBRATE

People have celebrations for all types of reasons. The most popular being a birthday. You lived another year, so celebrate! Anniversaries are also very popular. Celebrations occur for big events like weddings and babies as well. It is important for us to show the people we love that we support and care about them.

If this is the case, why not celebrate along the way when we have a long-term goal? It is good to have short-term celebrations to keep motivated. Celebrate throughout the entire journey when you complete significant milestones, for example when you complete your first 30 days of savings.

Celebrate the fact that after six months you are still keeping up your maintenance plan and continue to reward for yourself on a regular basis (I recommend every 2 to 3 months). Get yourself something you have been wanting for a while (that you can afford of course) and enjoy! You deserve it!

CONGRATULATIONS! You have everything in place that you need to achieve your goals and the process to manage any long-term goal you want to achieve in your life! You put in all the hard work, and now you just need to maintain it to achieve it.

CHAPTER 10

IN CONCLUSION

We have covered a lot in these few pages. How to create goals, how to create a financial plan, how to pay off debt, how to make yourself successful by having an accountability partner, being sure to celebrate your achievements and so much more.

I would like conclude this book by reminding you that just like physical fitness, financial fitness is a journey and not a destination. It requires constant monitoring and control of your behaviors. If you eat candy, cakes and pies every day with no vegetables and never work out your health will suffer. The same applies here. If you spend haphazardly and do not track your expenses, if you fail to pay yourself first or save to the do the fun things you want to do in life you will live in debt and may even have a poor credit score which costs you more money in the long run due to high interest rates for people with low or no credit histories.

I cannot stress enough that you do not have to go this alone. If you do not feel comfortable sharing your financial challenges with someone close to you, share it with us. We will keep your information confidential and work with you to come up with solutions to improve your overall financial health over time. We have all been in a bad spot at some point in our lives including me. It is an honor and a privilege to be able to give back to others.

I wish you nothing but success in your journey.

Heather Schooler

CHAPTER 11

BONUS INTERVIEW

As a bonus to you who purchased this book I am providing a copy of my interview with Kimberly Ivory Graves author of the book "Leaving Peace and Order" which helps people prepare for the transition of their loved ones. If you get a copy of her book from her website or contact her directly, please let her know that you got her information from The Money Library.

Heather: Hi, this is Heather Schooler from the Money Library, and today I am going to do an interview with an expert in final life arrangement Kimberly Graves, the author of "*Leaving Peace and Order.*" This is a fabulous book that talks about how to prepare for family and for loved ones and what to have in place for when they move on from this world into the next life that we have. So welcome, Kim. Thank you for joining me today.

Kimberly: Thank you, Heather. It is my pleasure to be here with you today.

Heather: I know I gave a brief introduction, but can you tell me a little bit more about you and what your company does?

Kim: Sure, I would be glad to. My name is, as Heather mentioned, Kimberly Ivory Graves. I am the author of "*Leaving Peace and Order: A Step-by-Step Guide to Getting Your Affairs in Order.* In *Leaving Peace and Order*", I encourage individuals to gather, record, and store their pertinent information as well as their final wishes in one place so that their loved ones can handle their arrangements and affairs with ease.

Along with my book, I created a companion workbook to make it easy to document your information. For more information about my book, you can visit ivoryspossibilties.com. Secondly I am the founder of the Peace and Order Academy, a one-stop shop legacy to launch in 2017.

At the Peace and Order Academy, we will empower and educate individuals on how to leave their loved ones an even more substantial legacy of wealth, peace, and order. We will partner with experts to offer professional workshops and online trainings covering the top four important aspects of life and end-of-life planning. These four are financial planning, insurance planning, estate planning, and end-of-life planning. So that is the Peace and Order Academy.

Heather: Kim, that sounds really exciting. I am looking forward to seeing that launch in 2017. Can you tell me a little bit about why you decided to start this type of business? Nothing I have seen in the marketplace has touched this, so it is a very unique offering. I was wondering why you got the idea and wanted to start the business.

Kim: You know, Heather, so often we hear and even experience loved ones passing away without having their affairs in order. Some do not have life insurance or even an adequate amount to cover their burial expenses. There is no living will or trust or even a will or anything like that, and even families are bickering over properties and belongings. It is just chaos when a loved one passes. And this should not be. So Peace and Order Academy is the first service that will bring the top four life-planning agencies together, not only to offer their service but most importantly, to educate individuals on the importance of having each aspect in place prior to one's passing. I feel that when people are educated and informed in certain areas, they tend to make better decisions. I believe it is a very selfish act to not take the time to make sure your finances are in order, you have insurance, you have a will or a trust, and that you have made your final wishes known to your loved ones. The Peace and Order Academy will help you in these variants.

Heather: Sounds wonderful! I think you told me through this question what the specific problem your business is addressing, but could you elaborate on that a little bit more?

Kim: Heather, when people do not know or understand what is available to them, they often do nothing. And that includes not getting their finances in order, not understanding the difference between a term life insurance policy or a whole life insurance policy or even whether they should have a will or whether they have enough to have a trust.

The Peace and Order Academy will address these top stages of life planning. That is the financial planning, insurance planning, estate planning, and end-of-life planning. Once these areas are established and in place, individuals are able to leave their loved ones an even more substantial legacy of wealth, peace, and order.

Heather: Fantastic. If someone is ready to get started today, they are listening to this audio or they are reading my book, and they are saying, "Hey, I have not gotten my copy of *Leaving Peace and Order* in the mail yet." The have ordered it, but they wanted to go ahead and get started today, what would be the one thing you would recommend that they do to start to prepare for their transition?

Kim: I think besides having life insurance, I believe that it is important that individuals have a discussion with their loved ones and make their final wishes known, and once they get my book, *"Leaving Peace and Order"*, they can use it as an icebreaker to get that topic going with their loved ones.

So many times, family members are blindsided by grief that they really had no idea what their loved one's desires were prior to their passing, so having that discussion up front, being open and honest, even though it is not an easy topic to discuss is important. I know that for me, my mom was very open and honest about what she wanted and what she did not want. And as a result of that conversation, I was able to handle her affairs and I was honoring what she wanted, and it made it a lot easier to handle her arrangements and handle her affairs for me.

Heather: That sounds great. I appreciate you taking the time to talk to me about this very important topic, Kim.

Kim: Heather, thank you for this opportunity.

Heather: Thank you, too. I appreciate it and enjoyed this conversation.

For more information on Kimberly's book please visit her website at www.ivoryspossibilities.com

YOUR COMPLIMENTARY GRADUATION GIFT

For those of you who have purchased this book, I would like to thank you for taking the first steps toward your financial freedom. As a congratulations for finishing this book I am offering you a free gift!

To collect your gift go to:

www.HeatherDSchooler.com
or text
Heather#Library
to 26786

You will receive a complimentary audio file with additional tips on how to better your money life.

FOLLOW ME

Follow Heather and
The Money Library on
Facebook Twitter & Instagram
@TheMoneyLibrary

BOOK HEATHER
FOR YOUR
NEXT EVENT

To book Heather to speak at your event
contact us at:

www.HeatherDSchooler.net

ABOUT THE AUTHOR

Heather D Schooler was born & raised in Dayton Ohio. The daughter of a high school principal and librarian, Heather was taught from an early age the value of education and believes in lifelong learning.

Heather's desire for lifelong learning enabled her to utilize her self-taught financial skills and in 2006 she developed her first financial curriculum to educate the next generation. With a desire to teach people how to retire while having fun working toward retirement, her fresh approach to the money game encourages people to take risks, do what they love and start early enjoying life to the fullest extent possible. Her business, The Money Library, provides individual and group coaching, public speaking, in house training courses, and maintains a repository of training materials to educate the world on all things money.